FUTURE READY PROJECT SKILLS

FUTURE READY CREATIVE WRITING PROJECTS

LYRIC GREEN AND DANA MEACHEN RAU

Enslow Publishing
101 W. 23rd Street
Suite 240
New York, NY 10011
USA
enslow.com

Dana Meachen Rau would like to thank Kelly Sanders, literacy specialist, West District School, Farmington, Connecticut, and Christie Wall, third grade teacher, Lake Garda School, Burlington, Connecticut, for the helpful conversations during the writing of this book.

Published in 2018 by Enslow Publishing, LLC
101 W. 23rd Street, Suite 240 New York, NY 10011

Library of Congress Cataloging-in-Publication Data

Names: Green, Lyric, author. | Rau, Dana Meachen, 1971- author.
Title: Future ready creative writing projects / Lyric Green and Dana Meachen Rau.
Description: New York : Enslow Publishing, 2018. | Series: Future ready project skills | Includes bibliographical references and index. | Audience: Grade 4 to 6.
Identifiers: LCCN 2017001293| ISBN 9780766086531 (library-bound) | ISBN 9780766087675 (pbk.) | ISBN 9780766087682 (6-pack)
Subjects: LCSH: Creative writing--Juvenile literature. | English language--Composition and exercises.
Classification: LCC LB1576 .G7397 2018 | DDC 372.62/3—dc23
LC record available at https://lccn.loc.gov/2017001293
Printed in China

To Our Readers: We have done our best to make sure all websites in this book were active and appropriate when we went to press. However, the author and the publisher have no control over and assume no liability for the material available on those websites or on any websites they may link to. Any comments or suggestions can be sent by e-mail to customerservice@enslow.com.

Portions of this book originally appeared in the book *Ace Your Creative Writing Project!*

Photo Credits: Cover, p. 1 ESB Basic/Shutterstock.com; p. 3 David Arts//Shutterstock.com; pp. 4, 11, 17, 26, 33, 42 Pressmaster/Shutterstock.com; p. 5 Adam Tinney/Shutterstock.com; p. 7 Topic Images Inc./Getty Images; p. 8 Westend61/Getty Images; p. 10 John Howard/DigitalVision/Getty Images; p. 12 Matt Carey/Moment/Getty Images; pp. 13, 16 (background), 21, 23, 38, 44 vvlinkov/Shutterstock.com (adapted); p. 14 Ana Blazic Pavlovic/ Shutterstock.com; p. 16 Dann Tardif/Corbis/Getty Images; p. 18 dimitris_k/Shutterstock.com; p. 19 Luisa Fumi/ Shutterstock.com; p. 22 Mark Segal/DigitalVision/Getty Images; p. 24 Hero Images/Getty Images; p. 27 © Ridofranz/iStock/Thinkstock; p. 29 MivPiv/E+/Getty Images; p. 31 © Stockbyte/Thinkstock; p. 34 Jovanmandic/ iStock/Thinkstock; p. 40 © iStockphoto.com/fstop123; p. 41 BeeBright/Shutterstock.com; p. 43 Blend Images - Moxie Productions/Brand X Pictures/Getty Images.

CONTENTS

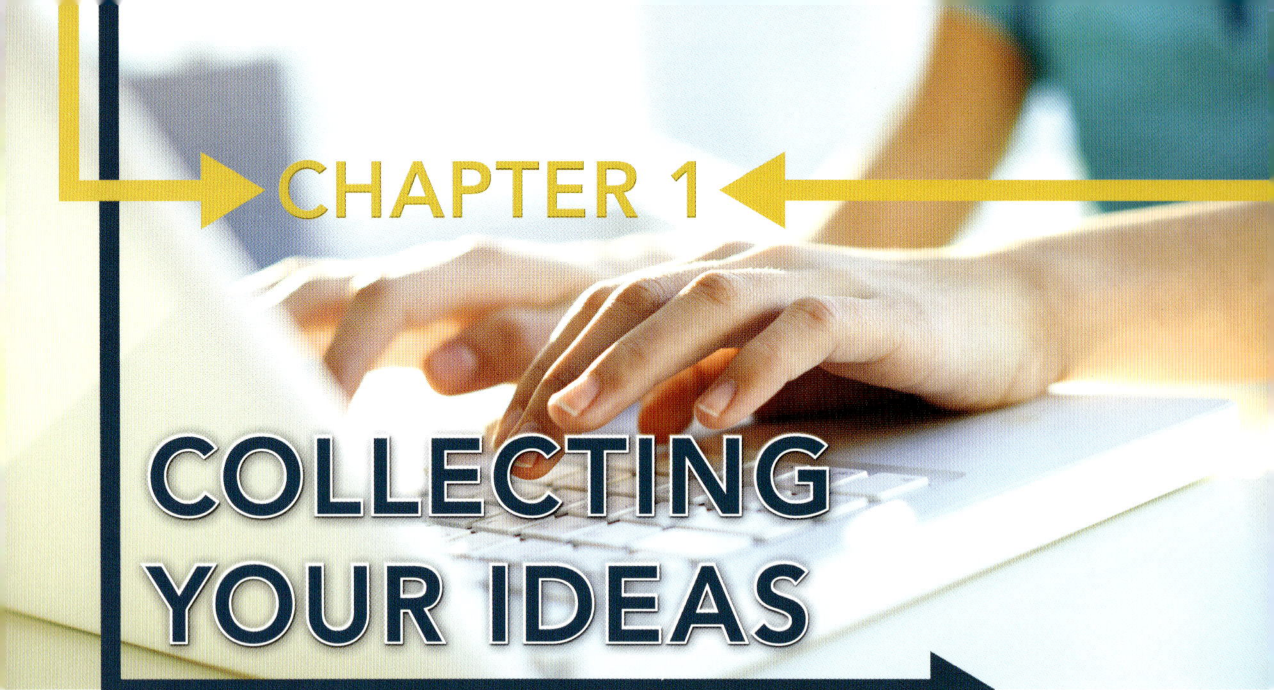

CHAPTER 1

COLLECTING YOUR IDEAS

Imagine that you have just spent a day at the beach. The sun is beginning to set, so it's time to go home. You have to gather all of your things. First you may pick up the beach blanket. The fabric is soft, but it's covered in rough sand. You found a smooth blue stone at one part of the beach and a spiral white shell in the water. Maybe you even found some sea glass or a bumpy piece of coral.

Collecting writing ideas is just like collecting items in your bag. As a writer, you are always carrying an invisible bag. Every experience you have, every person you meet, and every place you go can be an idea for creative writing. You can keep all of these ideas in your bag. Then they are handy when you need them.

Writing is an adventure! Just like you may collect shells on a beach or interesting leaves from a forest, you can collect ideas for writing.

GETTING CREATIVE

Creative writing is any writing that is meant to entertain readers. There are three main types of creative writing:

1. A personal narrative tells about an experience in your own life.
2. A fiction story is a story you make up.
3. A poem has many forms. Poets try to use words in a creative way to communicate a feeling or idea. They might tell a story or describe an object in simple words. Some poems have rhythm and rhyme like a song.

It is up to an author to choose the best type of creative writing to share their ideas. Sometimes an idea is best expressed using a certain type of creative writing.

Let's say that you want to write about a forest. In a personal narrative, one sentence might go like this:

There were birch trees as far as the eye could see.

This sentence could easily be part of a fiction story:

The birch trees bowed down as the snow giant passed them.

Or, these lines could be part of a poem:

Tall, thin tree
With white bark
And golden leaves in the fall.

GETTING STARTED

Collect everyday experiences. Don't worry if you've never been to the moon or met your favorite actor. Small

You can find inspiration anywhere. Everywhere you go, look for things that interest you or make you think.

experiences make good ideas, too. You can write about walking your dog in the park. You can tell a funny story about a disastrous attempt to bake cookies. You can even tell a story about folding your socks!

Always be on the lookout for new experiences. If someone asks you to go sailing, give it a try. You might love it! Your first time on the boat could make a great story. Even if you hate it, that would be a great story, too! Every experience you collect could be used for a personal narrative.

Also be sure to fill your bag with something that every writer carries—imagination. You could turn your real experiences into fictional ones. Maybe instead of walking a dog,

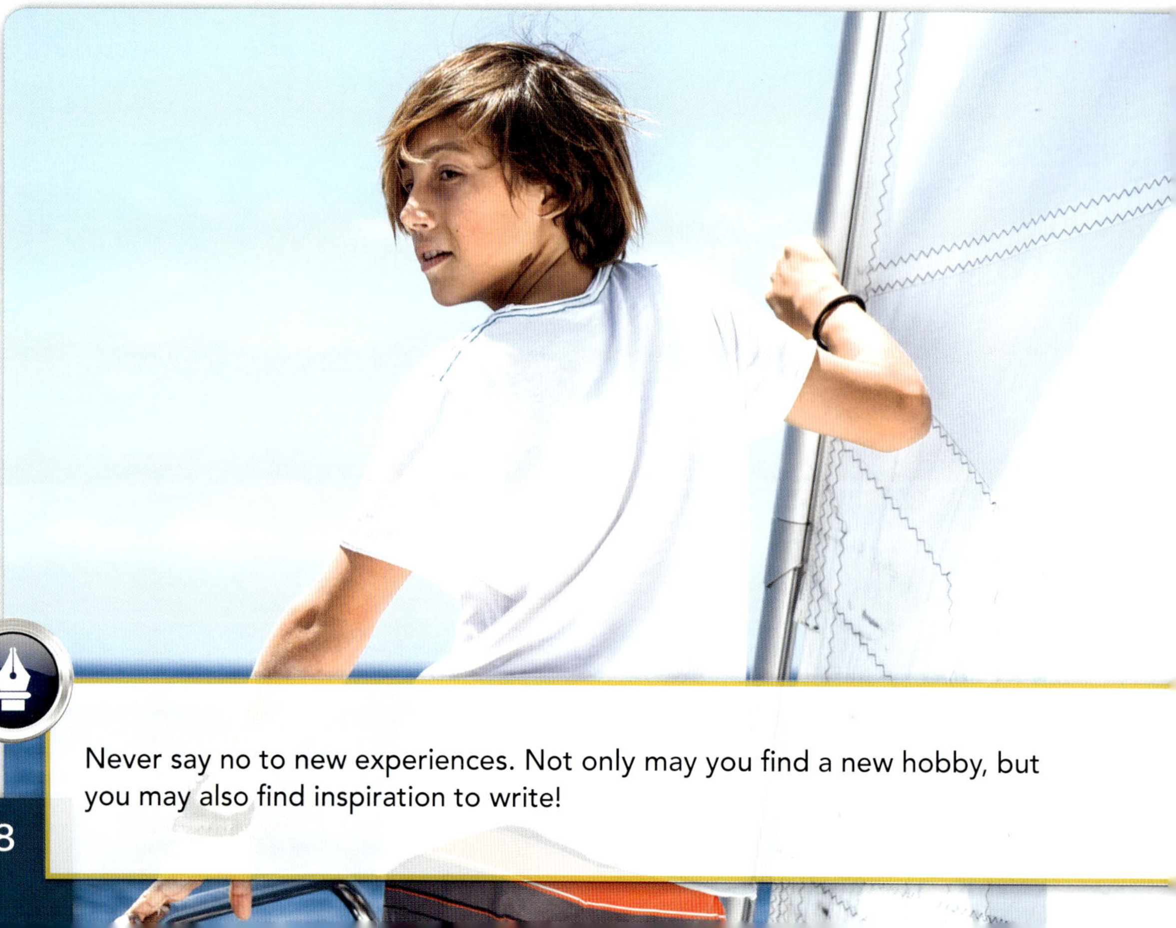

Never say no to new experiences. Not only may you find a new hobby, but you may also find inspiration to write!

you're taking your pet dragon for a walk! Or maybe while you're folding socks, one of them comes to life!

Let's say you want to write a poem. Reach into your bag and find one item or moment. A great bike ride on a beautiful day or a worn-out baseball glove will give you plenty of details to describe in your writing. Every new experience gives you writing ideas.

CONQUERING THAT SCARY BLANK PAGE

You wouldn't think an innocent piece of blank paper could be scary. But it can be terrifying for a writer without any ideas! Here are some ways to get your creativity flowing.

MAKE A LIST

One word can lead to an idea. Write down ten words that pop into your head. Then go back and circle the one that is most interesting to you. Maybe you wrote down pizza because you're hungry. Why not write about making the world's largest pizza?

Two words can also lead to an idea. Compare and contrast two different things. How is your cat like a marshmallow? Are they both soft and white? That might make a funny poem.

A PICTURE CAN INSPIRE A THOUSAND WORDS

A picture can lead to an idea, too. Flip through magazines with pictures of people. Think of them as characters. Ask

Keep a notebook handy for when inspiration strikes. You may not begin to write immediately, but later you'll be glad you saved that idea!

yourself questions about what they might be saying. What do you think their lives are like?

Not every writer meets the same people, goes to the same places, or does the same activities. Every writer works a little differently. As you keep reading this book, though, you'll see that all writers follow a similar process from idea to finished piece.

Write your ideas down if you think you'll forget about them. Even if they don't help you write something now, you never know what you might use later.

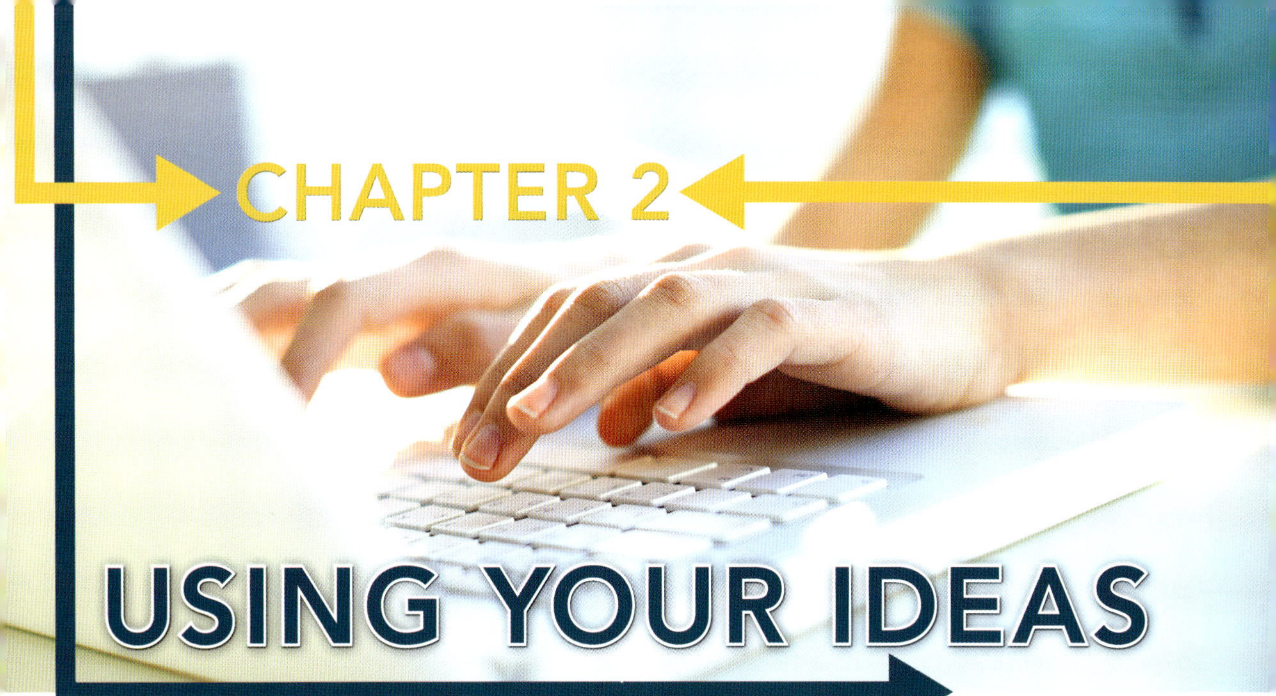

CHAPTER 2

USING YOUR IDEAS

It's time to dump out your bag. You've collected a pile of ideas, and now it's time to put them together for your reader.

Many writers start this process by asking themselves a question. They ask, "What's the best way to share my idea?" Do you want to describe a sunset you saw yesterday? A poem might be the best form of creative writing to use. Use personal narrative to tell about the time you lost your ball during a game. An idea about a pigeon who wants to sing on Broadway might work best as a fiction story.

OTHER TOOLS YOU NEED TO WRITE

Many pieces of writing need characters, a setting, and a plot. Characters are who is in the story. The setting is where the story takes place. The plot is what happens in the story. Your

Your writing bag will help you keep track of your ideas. It will also help you to create writing projects that reflect your own ideas and experiences.

piece also needs a beginning, a middle, and an end. All types of creative writing must include details.

You can start your piece by prewriting. Prewriting is making a writing plan. (The prefix pre- means "before," so prewriting means "before writing.") A great way to begin is to use graphic organizers. A graphic organizer is like a picture. It helps you organize your thoughts.

Let's say you want to write a personal narrative about getting ready for a party. A problem and solution chart could help you make your writing plan.

PROBLEM AND SOLUTION CHART

PROBLEM: I made cupcakes for my cousin's birthday, but I don't have any frosting.

SOLUTION:

- looked up recipes in my grandmother's cookbook and watched a video online
- found all of the ingredients
- made frosting from scratch

RESULT: I finished frosting the cupcakes just as my cousin came over!

For a fiction story, you can use a 5W chart to plan your characters, setting, and plot. The 5 Ws are often used by many writers to help create their stories. Don't worry about writing complete sentences. Just write a few words that will help you remember your ideas later.

5W CHART

Who? **(characters)** twin brother and sister
What? **(plot)** get lost
When? **(setting)** at night
Where? **(setting)** in the woods
Why? **(detail)** because it's dark

As you prewrite, it is important to think about the theme of your piece. Your theme is your main message. What do you want readers to learn from your story or poem? For example, what would be the theme of a

Be sure to give yourself time to think about your writing piece. How do you want your readers to feel when they read it? What do you want them to learn about your characters or story? What are you trying to say with your piece?

personal narrative about your first day at baseball camp? It could be bravery, or maybe even fear. What if you're planning on writing a poem about the apple tree in your front yard? The theme might be sweetness since the blooms smell sweet, and the fruit they create is also sweet.

DRAFTING

Not all writers make a prewriting plan. Some just start drafting. Jane Yolen, a famous author, says, "I generally do not think out plots or characters ahead of time. I let things roll along. . . . I want my own writing to surprise me."

Remember though—Jane Yolen is a professional author. She has been writing for a long time and has written many books and stories. For beginning writers, prewriting can be really useful. It can help you check that your story has all the important parts or that your poem says everything you want it to say.

As you write down your ideas, your plan will start to take shape. It's okay if your first draft is messy. At this point, don't even worry about perfect spelling. After you have a draft, you'll go on to revising. Revising is when you add words, take words away, and change details to make your piece better. One draft is never enough—even for famous authors. Award-winning author Gail Carson Levine believes that "the best way to write better is to write more."

THE WRITER'S PROCESS

1. **PREWRITING:** organizing your thoughts and making a writing plan
2. **DRAFTING:** creating the first version of your story, narrative, or poem
3. **REVISING:** making your piece better
4. **PEER REVIEW:** getting feedback from other writers
5. **PUBLISHING:** sharing your work with readers

The writing process can be fun. It may seem hard to have to draft and revise, but when you finish your piece, you'll feel proud of what you've done.

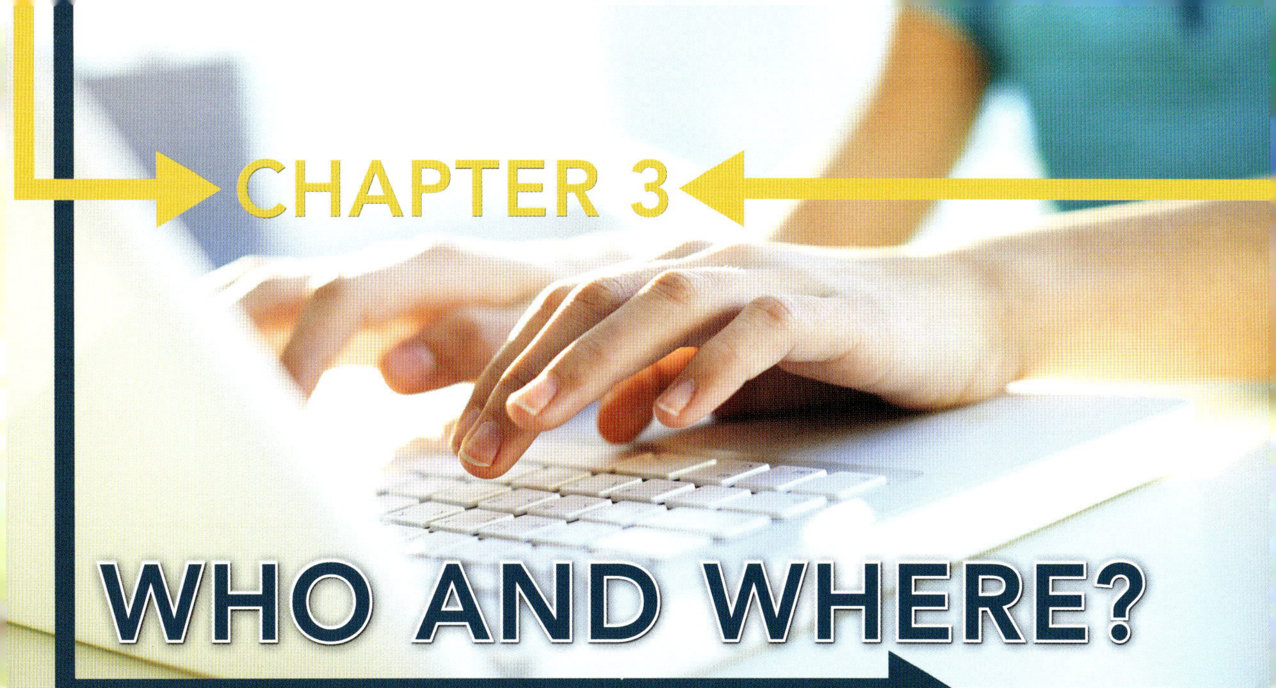

CHAPTER 3
WHO AND WHERE?

Characters can be people, such as Max in *Where the Wild Things Are* by Maurice Sendak. They can also be animals, such as Wilbur the pig in E.B. White's *Charlotte's Web*. Characters can even be objects, such as Winnie the Pooh, or something in nature, such as the tree in Shel Silverstein's *The Giving Tree*. There are many types of characters, and not all pieces of writing will use every type. But there are certain types of characters that are important to most stories.

THE NARRATOR

The narrator of a story is the person telling the story. The narrator may be a character in the story—but not always. In a personal narrative, you will probably be both the main character and the narrator. For a fiction story, you make up your own

A busy park or street can inspire you. Look at all the different people you see. Imagine their lives. Where are they going? What do they do for fun? Anyone can be a character in your creative writing!

narrator and characters. You get to choose names for them. You also decide how they look, act, and feel. Poems may have characters, too. Shel Silverstein, the poet who wrote *Where the Sidewalk Ends*, often writes poems with characters.

If you need character ideas, check your bag. Characters can be based on people you know. They can be based on strangers, too. Author Kate DiCamillo says, "Writing is seeing. It is paying attention." Why not sit on a park bench and watch families go by? Ask yourself questions as you watch. Why is that man in such a hurry? What made that girl smile? Why is that boy wearing that jacket? What is that woman carrying in her purse? Then you can make up stories to answer your questions.

BRINGING YOUR CHARACTERS TO LIFE

Open your bag again. Look through your ideas and experiences to find details about your characters. Some writers "interview" their characters. They create a character sketch. A character sketch helps you get to know who you are writing about. Simply write down some details about your character, such as name, age, family, and where they were born. The more details you know about your character, the more real your characters will seem to your reader. Even if these details don't make it into your story, they will show in your writing.

What are your hobbies? Is there something that you can do that no one else can? Is there something that makes you happy? Write about those things!

In your creative writing, try not to just tell readers what a character is like. It is boring to read, "Henry was a smart boy." It is better to show your characters' personalities. Write about what a character actually says and does. Dialogue can show your reader what your characters are like. If your character says, "Out of my way!" you are showing that he is gruff and bossy. But if your character says, "Excuse me, please. Do you mind moving aside? I need to get by," he is polite and respectful.

Also show your characters' behavior—what they do. "Veronica was hungry" might be true. But instead, try "Veronica shoved the cookie into her mouth in one bite. Then she took a gulp of milk before she even finished chewing." In the second example, you are showing your reader that Veronica is hungry. You never even have to use the word hungry.

Here's an example from a personal narrative. It only tells the reader how the narrator feels: *Even though I am growing up, I still care about the stuffed bear I slept with when I was a baby.*

Your writing will be much better if you show the feeling through words and actions. Here is a revised example:

I was cleaning my room when I spotted my stuffed bear on the floor. I picked up Goffy and fluffed her purple hair. "You poor thing!" I said. "I'll find a better spot for you!" I cleared a place next to my paint set and sat Goffy on the shelf near my bed.

This example shows—instead of tells—readers that the narrator cares about his bear.

CHARACTER SKETCH

Use these questions to write details about your characters. Copy the questions onto a separate piece of paper and add your answers.

- What is the name and age of my character?
- What does my character look like?
- What does he or she like to do? What does he or she not like to do?
- What is my character's favorite color, book, food, and song?
- Who are my character's friends?
- What do other people think of my character?
- What does my character keep in his or her desk at school?

Remember that these questions are only examples. You can "ask" your characters anything you want to know about them. Their answers might surprise you!

SETTING

Setting is where and when your narrative, story, or poem happens. Look in your bag. Take out your collection of all the places you've been. Maybe you spent a vacation on a farm or went on a road trip with your family. Other settings could be school, an attic or basement, and even the inside of a car. You

Do you like to travel? Maybe you've been somewhere that your classmates or friends haven't. Remember that anywhere can be a setting, and the clearer your setting is to you, the clearer it will be to your readers.

can also wonder about places you've never seen but want to visit, such as Egypt or the moon. Try to imagine a place long ago in history, such as a German castle or a horse and buggy in the Wild West.

As you plan your setting, think about the mood you want to create. The mood is the feeling that your reader gets from your writing. If your setting is a spooky house, use words that make it sound spooky. Don't describe how the walls are gray or that the lights are off. Instead, talk about the cobwebs on the chandeliers or the shadows that darkened every corner.

As you add details, don't just think about how the setting looks. What about your other senses? How does it smell? How does it feel to be there? Use a graphic organizer to brainstorm for setting details.

Also ask yourself when your piece takes place. Are you writing about your grandmother taking you to the symphony last summer? Then your setting is in the past. The present means the story is happening right now. Are you writing about what life will be like in a hundred years? Do your characters wear hover sneakers and use robots to do their homework? Then your setting is the future!

BRAINSTORMING A SETTING

SETTING: Inside my treehouse
I see the wooden floor.
I hear the birds singing in the next tree.
It smells damp since it just rained.
I taste the brownie I ate as a snack.
I feel the soft rug my mother let me have for the floor.

RESEARCH: FILLING UP YOUR BAG

The setting of your writing might be sometime in history. Or you might want to write about something scientific. This means you'll have to do some research. Head to the library. Check out books about your topic. You can also do research on the Internet looking for reliable sources, such as online science or history journals, newspapers, or online encyclopedias. When you do research online, you have to be careful. An adult can help you decide what sites are safe for you to visit. If a website asks you to enter any personal information—such as your name, age, address, or photograph—go to another site.

When you use new information, you have to be careful to write it in your own words. Plagiarism is taking someone

Be sure and read your writing. As you do, you may find areas where you want to add more detail or take out details. You may also find words you've misspelled or places where your tense doen't make sense.

else's words or ideas and calling them your own. Plagiarism is against the law.

TENSE MATTERS

It is important to think about the tense of your verbs. The time of your story—the past, present, or future—will help you figure out what tense to use.

Past tense: Charlie ate hot dogs for dinner last night.
Present tense: Charlie eats hot dogs for lunch.
Future tense: Charlie will eat hot dogs for dinner—if there are any left!

Tense is very important. If you don't use the right tense, your sentence won't make sense. (That's a rhyme that will help you remember!) Charlie cannot ate hot dogs tomorrow for lunch.

CHAPTER 4

AND THEN WHAT HAPPENED?

Your characters might be interesting and your setting might be exotic, but you need a good plot, too. Your reader will lose interest if nothing really happens! A story's plot has a beginning, a buildup, a climax, and an ending. Most stories have a main problem that the main character tries to solve over the course of the plot.

A BOLD BEGINNING

A good story starts with a bold beginning. First, you need to make your readers want to read more. Then you have to provide some background. In the beginning, you will introduce your characters and the setting. You should also introduce the story's main problem.

Here is an example of a story's beginning. It tells us what the story will be about, but it doesn't make you want to keep reading:

Keeping your readers interested will require an interesting plot. Make sure that something happens to your characters and that they react in a way that is believable and unique to them.

I got new snow boots for Christmas.

You can spice up a beginning by using dialogue. For example, show your character's feelings right away:

"Thanks, Mom," I said as I put the new snow boots aside. I was much more excited about the new Mario Kart game I'd received. Sitting by the tree and surrounded by wrapping paper, going outside was the last thing I was thinking about.

"Don't you want to try them on, Matt?" Mom asked. I noticed she was already wearing the new snow boots Dad had

gotten her. "Look outside before you answer." Groaning, I stood up and walked toward the window.

In this beginning, we meet the characters: a boy who is excited for his new video game and a mother is who is more excited about snow boots. We see the setting: Christmas morning. We can also see a problem: mother and son want to do different things on Christmas morning. This beginning leaves the reader with more questions. Why is Matt's mom wearing her snow boots? What will be outside the window?

Starting in the middle of the plot can also be a good way to pull readers right into the scene:

Samantha raced as fast as she could toward home base. The coach waved her in, but the other player was rushing closer with the ball to tag her.

Look at how much we learn in just two sentences. Already we know the main character (Samantha), the setting (a softball game), and the problem (getting to home base in time).

A SUSPENSEFUL BUILDUP

In the buildup of your story, your character tries to solve the problem. You can do this by creating suspense. Suspense is when you can't wait to find out what happens. For example, let's say your main character is worried that his friend will never call. That's his problem. What's the story? The phone rings, but it's his grandmother. It rings again, and it's his cousin. It rings again, but it's his dad. Readers will be in suspense as they wait for the call along with the character.

AN EXCITING CLIMAX

The climax is the most important or exciting moment of the story. At the climax, the reader finds out how the problem gets solved. For example, a climax could be when a rescue crew arrives to save a group of lost hikers. Or the main character finally scores a goal to win the soccer tournament in overtime. Take time to describe this moment. Help your readers picture the action as it happens.

Creating a story can be like climbing a mountain. The buildup is similar to the actions you take while you're climbing. The climax is the top of the mountain.

Perhaps a character named Riley has been trying to think of ways to cheer up her sick brother Sam. She's tried everything—chicken soup, a stuffed animal, and a homemade card. The following example is the climax of this story. But it is not very exciting.

Sam just wanted Riley to keep him company.

Take some time to make the moment more exciting. Have Riley sit down on Sam's bed. Describe the quilt. Then describe how Riley feels and what she says to Sam. Describe Sam's expression and what he says to Riley. Show how much they care about each other by the way they act.

A SATISFYING ENDING

A story may not be over because the problem is solved. In the ending, the reader often learns what happens after the climax. Don't end the story too quickly. The events of the story have probably changed your main character. Tell your readers how your character feels or what your character will do with the lesson he or she has learned.

The following ending doesn't show what your character experienced in the story:

I put on my pajamas and went to bed.

This ending shows the reader that the character has definitely changed:

As I went to bed, I thought, "I will never try to dress up my dog in doll clothes again!"

POEMS

Poetry doesn't always have a plot. Some poems just describe something, such as a character, setting, object, or moment. Like personal narratives and fiction stories, poems also have themes and moods. With just a few words, poets create a snapshot in a reader's mind. Some poems may only be two lines long. Others may have two hundred lines! Personal narratives and fiction stories use paragraphs to break up the story. Many poems use groups of lines called stanzas.

Writing poems can be a great way to express thoughts, feelings, or even stories. Many famous novel writers also write poetry.

Rhyme, rhythm, and repetition can really spice up a poem. Rhyme is the use of the same sound in more than one word, such as bake and cake. Rhythm is when lines have a particular beat like music. Repetition means using the same words over and over.

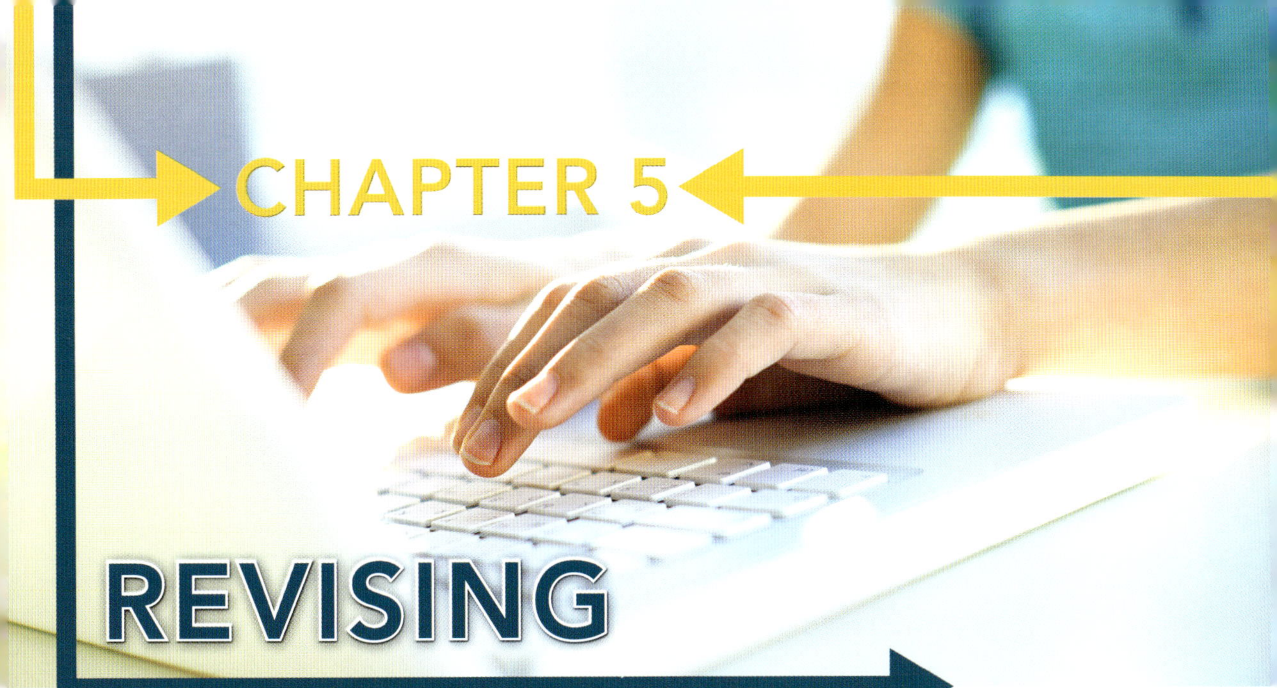

CHAPTER 5

REVISING

Revision can be the most fun part of creative writing. It is like playing with modeling clay. Everything you need is there—the characters, setting, and story. But it is just a blob. With revision you can make it into something readers can understand. This is when you can really make your story good.

GIVE MORE DETAILS

Adding more details is an important way to revise. This is called expanding your writing. You can also revise by taking out words. This is called tightening. Replace some words with better ones. Revising means making your piece the best it can be.

Some people like to listen to music while they draft or revise. It can help set a mood and can also help you concentrate!

EXPANDING

First, look for places to expand with details. The more details you give your reader, the more real your story or poem will become. You might have a picture in your head as you write. Did you give enough detail for your reader to see the same picture?

Maybe you wrote a personal narrative about your trip to the shoe store. You included this sentence:

I saw lots of shoes.

This is a good place to add more details to describe the shoes you saw. Ask yourself questions. What types of shoes did you see? What did they look like? Where could they be worn? Who was buying the shoes?

This expanded description is better:

The store was filled with hundreds of shoes. There were brightly colored sneakers for running. There were boots with thick soles for stomping and high heels with sparkles for dancing.

Details can also tell you more about a character. Don't just add any details, though. You always have to think about the mood and theme of your piece of writing.

This sentence doesn't tell us much about the character or what he is going to say:

The principal stood in front of the room. He had something to tell the children.

Details can tell us more about the principal. Here is an example with more details:

The principal wore a gray jacket and a blue tie. He had a silver watch and wore thick glasses. He stood in front of the room. He had something to tell the children.

The details above don't tell us about the principal's personality or his news for the children.

If you add the right details, readers learn a lot more:

The principal stood in front of the room with his arms folded at his chest. He cleared his throat and glared at the children.

With just a couple new details, we have a scary principal with bad news to share.

Other details create the opposite picture:

The principal waved at the children as they entered. He had a huge smile on his face as he stood in front of the room.

Now we've created a friendly principal with good news to share!

DIALOGUE

As you revise, you decide the best way to tell your story. Are you only using characters' thoughts to tell the story? Or will the characters speak to each other in dialogue? Many good stories have a mixture of both. Let's say your story includes this sentence:

Gabby forgot to put the lid on the blender before mixing a milk shake.

Revise this section by using dialogue instead.

"Could you pass the chocolate?" Gabby asked.
Max gave her the bar. "What do you need it for?"
"I want to put it in the blender," she said.
"Why do you want to put chocolate in a blender?" Max asked.
"Chocolate milk shakes!" Gabby pressed the button.
"You forgot to put the top on!" Max exclaimed.
"Could you hand me a towel?" Gabby asked.

This dialogue tells us what Gabby is doing and what Max thinks about it. The writer doesn't say Gabby makes a mess. But we know she does because she asks for a towel.

COLORFUL COMPARISONS

You can use special writing techniques to make your writing more colorful. Comparing two unlike things is one way. Venn diagrams can help you make comparisons. Perhaps you wrote a story about how crazy your classmates are. When you revise, think about what you could compare them to. Maybe a bunch of monkeys?

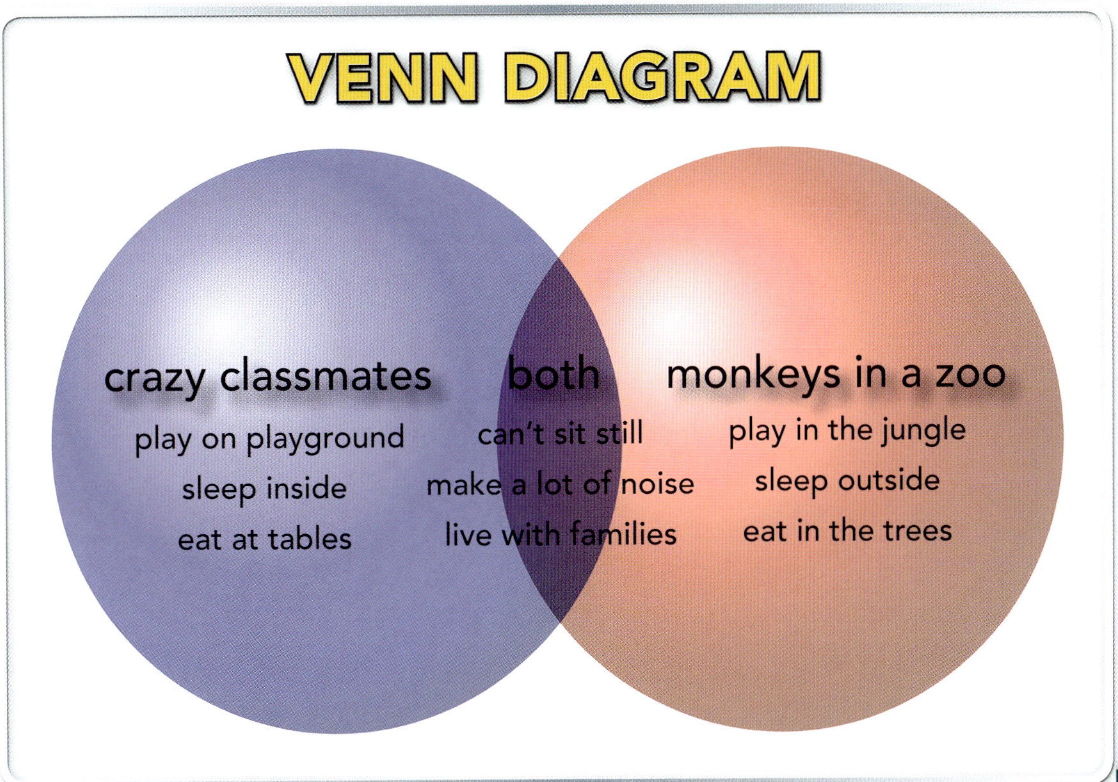

Poets often use similes and metaphors to create images in their readers' minds. Both describe an object, person, or place as something else entirely. But a simile uses the words "like" or "as" in the description:

Spaghetti's swirly, curly, and twirly like a bowl of wiggly worms. (simile)

Warily I wind my fork in the bowl of worms wiggling in spaghetti sauce. (metaphor)

OTHER HELPFUL WRITING TECHNIQUES

ALLITERATION: repeating the first sound in a word. *Silly salamanders scamper.*

PERSONIFICATION: talking about an object as if it is a person. *The wind howled.* (The wind is howling like a wolf. The wind doesn't really howl.)

HYPERBOLE: exaggerating the truth. *The ship was as big as a city!*

TIGHTENING YOUR WORDS

Adding words can help make your writing more fun. But tightening is important, too. Take out unnecessary words, sentences, or images. If they are not important, they are probably in the way. Sometimes the most powerful sentences are those with only two or three words.

As a writer, you always make choices. Decide on the main idea of each scene. Then decide if all the details in that scene relate to your idea. For example, this writer wanted the action to be fast. She needed to keep up the pace. You can see where she deleted some words.

The ~~large wooden~~ ship rushed toward the shore ~~of the island~~. ~~The island had palm trees, green grass, and black rocks~~. The captain had to steer clear of the rocks, or the ship would crash. ~~He ran around the deck and shouted out orders.~~ He grabbed the wheel and pulled hard ~~to make the ship turn in the other direction~~. The rocks rushed closer ~~as wind blew on the sails and sent the boat toward the rocks~~. The crew scurried on deck and pulled down the sails. With one last yank, the captain turned the boat ~~away from the shore~~. A rock scraped the ship, but it ~~only left a long line along the side and~~ didn't break through. The captain sighed and walked back to the crew. The crew cheered ~~because they were so happy~~. They were safe.

After expanding and tightening, look at your words. Find general, nondescriptive words and replace them with more specific ones. Look at this sentence:

Colorful flowers grew in the garden.

"Colorful," "flowers," and "grew" are very general words. They don't show the reader exactly what the garden looks like.

Can you make the words more specific? Are the flowers roses? Irises? What color are the flowers? Are there a lot or just a few? This sentence creates a better picture for the reader:

Yellow sunflowers towered over the garden.

PROOFREADING

An important part of the revising process is proofreading. This is when you check your piece for mistakes in grammar, spelling, and punctuation. You can use a dictionary to look up the

After you have drafted your piece, revise it to make it better. Revisit the place where you got inspired if you can, and make sure all of your sentences are clear to your readers.

Proofreading is a very important part of the writing process. You can find spelling and grammatical errors, as well as other mistakes you may have made while writing.

meaning of words. You can also use a thesaurus to find more descriptive words. Your computer has these tools, too.

You can check your spelling on the computer. Remember, though, that the computer spell check doesn't catch all mistakes. The words in the following sentence are spelled correctly, but some are the wrong words to use. The computer won't find the mistakes. Can you?

The kids red there books quietly.

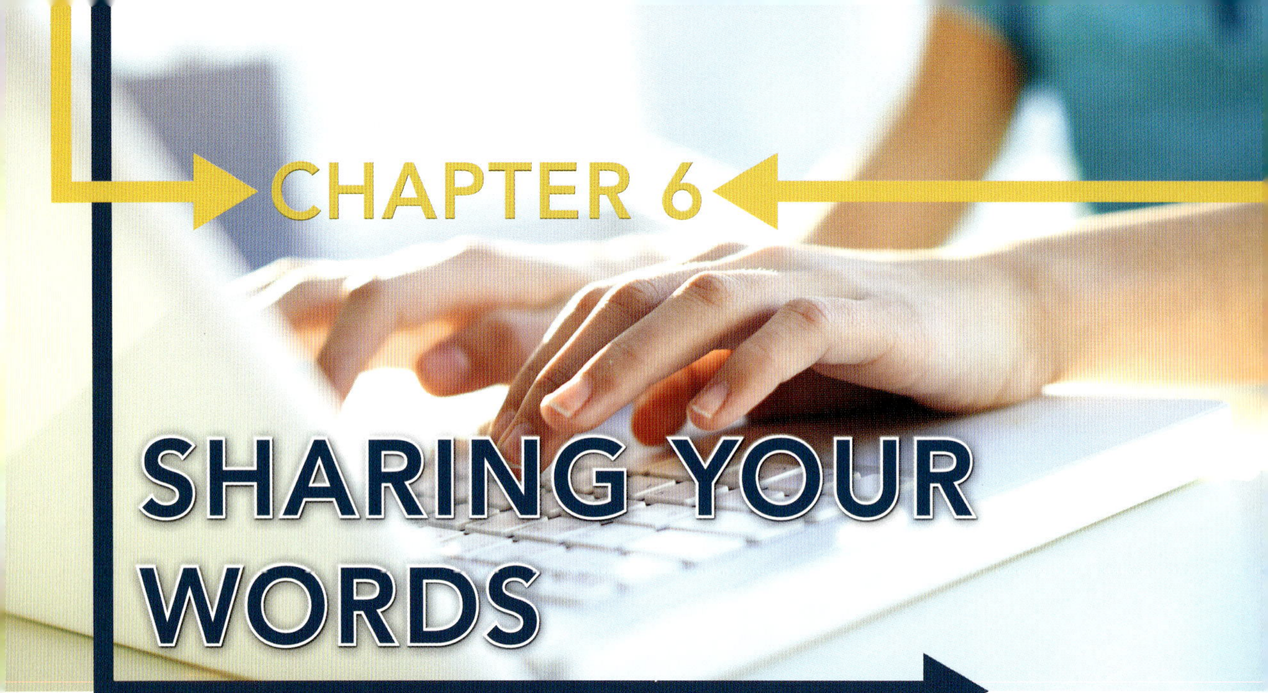

CHAPTER 6

SHARING YOUR WORDS

You don't have to keep the treasures in your bag a secret. You can give your readers a sneak peak! Don't wait until you are done writing to show someone else. Get some advice! Even professional authors don't write alone. They get advice from other writers during all steps of the process. Many authors bounce ideas around with a writing partner or partners. This can help you get new ideas for characters, plot, setting, or anything else! A writing partner can be a lifesaver.

PEER REVIEW

Peer review is when you trade papers with a classmate or friend or read your work to a group. Your partner or group's feedback will improve your writing.

A peer reviewer might point out something that worked well. She might say, "I could tell Joe was shy because he always hid in the closet." Then she'll point out ways to improve your story. She might say, "You said Annie was rich, so I wanted you

Sharing your work with friends can be fun and helpful! Your peers may find issues with your piece that you didn't. They may also observe great achievements that you may have missed!

to give me more details about her house and her clothes." A peer reviewer might also use a rubric. This is a list of requirements that your teacher expects from the assignment.

Giving other people feedback on their work helps you, too. It is a great way to practice being a writer. You learn what works and doesn't work. You can use what you learn the next time you write something.

After you get feedback, you might have to revise your work again. In fact, you'll probably need to revise many times before your piece is done. You may never feel like your piece is done. This is common for many authors.

Revising is practice. The more you write, the more practice you get. The more practice, the better your writing! Your

MAKE YOUR OWN BOOK!

1. Fold ten sheets of plain white paper in half. This will give you twenty blank pages in your book.
2. Fold one piece of colorful construction paper in half. This is your cover.
3. Slip the white pages inside the cover.
4. Secure the pages to the cover with a ribbon or staples.
5. Fill your book with your creative writing and share it with readers!

piece is done when you can't find any more mistakes and you feel your ideas are easy to understand.

PUBLISHING

Now it's time to share your ideas with the world. This is called publishing. You can entertain an audience by reading your piece aloud. You can give it to someone as a gift. Some kids get their work published in magazines. Websites post kids' stories, too. Always check with an adult to see if a site is safe. You can even make your work into a book and keep it on your shelf.

You don't have to share your work. It's okay if you want to write memories, stories, and poems just for yourself. A diary or journal is a great type of creative writing.

Now that you've emptied your bag, pick it up and head back out. It's time to collect some new ideas!

GLOSSARY

buildup The part of a story when the character struggles with a problem.

characters The people, animals, or objects in a story.

character sketch A description of a character's appearance and personality. This description helps a writer learn more about the character before starting to write.

climax The most important or exciting moment in the story when the problem or mystery is solved.

descriptive Using lots of details to tell exactly what someone or something is like.

dialogue Words that characters say when they speak directly to each other.

drafting Creating the first version of your piece of writing.

expanding Adding more information and details.

feedback Someone else's opinions or thoughts about your work.

fiction story Writing you make up with your imagination that is often in the form of sentences and paragraphs.

graphic organizers Charts and diagrams that writers use to plan and organize their work.

metaphor A comparison without using "like" or "as."

mood The feeling of a piece of writing, such as scary, silly, or sad.

narrator The character who tells the story.

peer review Sharing your work with other writers to see what they think.

personal narrative Writing that describes an experience in your own life.

plagiarism Using someone else's words as if they were your own without giving credit to the original writer or speaker.

plot What happens in a story.

prewriting Organizing your ideas before drafting your piece of writing.

proofreading Rereading your piece to fix spelling, grammar, and punctuation mistakes.

revising Adding, taking away, replacing, or moving words around to improve your piece of writing.

rubric A checklist that tells a writer what is expected from an assignment.

setting Where and when a story takes place.

similes Comparisons using the word "like" or "as."

suspense A feeling of wanting to know what happens next.

tense The form of a verb that tells readers if the action happens in the past, present, or future.

theme The main message or point of a piece of writing.

thesaurus A reference book or computer tool that lists a word along with other words that have the same or similar meaning.

tightening Taking out unnecessary words while revising.

FURTHER READING

BOOKS

826 Valencia. *642 Things to Write About—Young Writer's Edition*. San Francisco, CA: Chronicle Books, 2014.

Levine, Gail Carson. *Writer to Writer: From Think to Ink*. New York, NY: HarperCollins, 2014.

Levine, Gail Carson. *Writing Magic*. New York, NY: HarperCollins, 2014.

Snider, Brandon T. *Write It Out: Hundreds of Writing Prompts to Inspire Creative Thinking*. New York, NY: Sterling Publishing, 2016.

Strausser, Jeffery. *Barron's Painless Writing, 3rd Edition*. Hauppage, NY: Barron's, 2014.

WEBSITES

Grammar Man
grammarmancomic.com/comics/grammarman/
Read an online comic about English grammar.

Journal Buddies
journalbuddies.com/journal_prompts__journal_topics/fun-writing-prompts-for-middle-school/
Thirty-one fun writing prompts.

Time4Writing
http://www.time4writing.com/free-writing-resources/
Find many writing sources for students.

INDEX